Where We Live

Poland

Donna Bailey and Anna Sproule

RSVP
**RAINTREE
STECK-VAUGHN**
PUBLISHERS

Hello. My name is Manya, and
these are my brothers Jozef and Karol.
We live in a village in Poland.

Many people in our village own horses.
Some people ride to church every Sunday
in horse-drawn carts.

Dad is a farmer.

He grows wheat and potatoes on his farm.

In the spring he plows the land.

We have a horse to pull the plow.

4

When the ground is ready, Jozef and
our neighbors help Dad plant potatoes.
They load their baskets from the cart
and drop the little potatoes as they walk
along the plowed rows.

Later in the summer we all help
with the potato harvest.
Mom chooses the best potatoes to sell.
We keep the rest to eat in the winter.

It gets very hot in the summer, and
the grass in the meadows grows tall.
Dad cuts the grass and lets it dry in the sun.
It makes hay to feed the animals in the winter.

The hay is loaded onto wagons.
Then the horses pull the loaded wagons
back to the village.
It's fun to ride on top of the haystack!

The wagons have to cross a bridge
before they reach the village.
Sometimes there is a traffic jam
when two wagons meet on the bridge.

Later in the summer when the wheat harvest
is finished, there is a big harvest festival
in the village.
Someone is chosen to be Queen of the Harvest.
She dresses in her best clothes and
wears a crown made from ears of wheat.

Many people love to sing and dance, so
there is always music during
the harvest festival.
The musicians play their flutes
and violins.

We all wear traditional costumes and
dance traditional Polish dances.

In the fall the weather gets cold.
We stack wood for our winter fires
in the sheds by the farmyard.

During the winter, snow covers the ground.
If we run low on wood for the fire,
we must cut down more trees.

During the long, cold winter, people stay inside.
In southern Poland, people often use the
time to decorate their walls and furniture
with beautiful patterns.

This woman uses a pole to pull buckets of
water from the well.
She painted flowers on her buckets and
on the well in her yard.
She even decorated her tree!

These people live in the country near Warsaw.
Warsaw is the capital of Poland, but
these people live in a place called Lowicz.
They are wearing their traditional clothes.
The men wear black velvet jackets and
embroidered shirts.

Can you see the embroidery on
this woman's blouse?
Many people in the town of Lowicz
wear embroidery on their best clothes.
This woman made the lace
on her blouse, too.

The girls in Lowicz learn to embroider
when they are still at school.
They make many beautiful patterns
on skirts, shirts, and blouses.

In early summer during the festival of
Corpus Christi, people in Lowicz wear
their best clothes.
The small children carry baskets of flowers.
We all follow the priests in a procession
through the streets.

Young girls wear white dresses
and pin white flowers in their hair.
They follow the children and carry cushions.
On each cushion is a cross or holy object.

A man carrying a banner is followed by
the other people in the procession.
The procession stops at four places.
The priests say prayers at each stop.

Polish people also wear their beautiful
embroidered clothes to weddings.
These girls live in the Tatra Mountains
in southern Poland.
They are all going to be bridesmaids
at a wedding in the village.

Before the wedding, the bridesmaids make
the bride a crown of flowers and tinsel.
In the middle of the flowers, they put
a pair of shoes as a present to the bride.

On the day of the wedding, everyone goes
to the bride's house.
The bride does a dance, and everyone
gives her money for luck.

25

Soon it is time to go to the church.
The bride and groom ride to church in
a carriage pulled by two horses.
The bride's parents ride behind her in
another carriage.

At the church the bride and groom
kneel before the priest.
They each hold a lighted candle.
During the wedding ceremony, the groom
puts a ring on the bride's finger,
and she gives him a ring in return.

When the ceremony is finished, the bride
and groom stand at the door of the church.
Everyone wishes them good luck.

Then the wedding party walks through
the streets to the groom's family home.
Musicians walk in front of the bride and
groom and play their violins.

Then it is time for the wedding feast.

There is always plenty to eat and drink.

Everyone laughs and talks.

Afterward the bride and groom dance together.
The musicians play a traditional dance,
and everyone joins in.

Later in the evening, the bride is crowned
by her attendants.
The bride and groom then leave the party,
but the music and dancing continues.
Sometimes the party lasts for several days!

Index

Reading Consultant: Diana Bentley
Editorial Consultant: Donna Bailey
Supervising Editor: Kathleen Fitzgibbon

Illustrated by Anna Dzierzek/John Martin and Artists Ltd
Picture research by Suzanne Williams
Designed by Richard Garratt Design

Photographs:
Cover: Rex Features
Colorific: 3 and 14
Susan Griggs Picture Agency: 17 and 18 (Charles W. Friend)
Robert Harding Picture Library: 1, 8, 10, 11, 12, 15, 16, 20, 21, and 22
Rex Features: 4, 5, 26 and 27
Tim Sharman: 2, 9, 13, 19, 23, 28, 29, 30, 31 and 32

Library of Congress Cataloging-in-Publication Data: Bailey, Donna. Where we live—Poland/Donna Bailey and Anna
Sproule. p. cm. SUMMARY: Depicts the occupations, daily activities, festivals, and ceremonies of Poland. ISBN 0-8114-2556-
1. Poland—Social life and customs—Juvenile literature. [1. Poland—Social life and customs.] I. Sproule, Anna. II. Title.
DK4110.B35 1990 943.805′6—dc20 89-13358 CIP AC

2 3 4 5 6 7 8 9 LB 98 97 96 95 94

DATE DUE			
JAN 16 199 FEB 13 1998			
APR 30 1997			
MAY 09 1997			
MAY 16 1997			
MAY 30 1997			
JUN 06 1997 MY 28 98